For All The Midnight Dwellers

Claire Stuesse

i

DEDICATION

This book is dedicated to all my muses. Without you, I would be a fool with a pen and an empty page. Instead I am a fool with a pen and enough pages to fill a book.

AUTHORS NOTE;
This book is ordered like my mind, somewhat
random at first glance, but if you stay awhile and
look it through, you might find how each poem,
each thought, in some way connects to the next.

Not too Late to Turn Back

If I showed you my mind
Would you run and hide?
Or would you find
Something
That you could relate to?
Something
That resembled a piece of you
Would you get as far
As all my scars?
And leave
In the light of day
Or would you stay
Till the night
And search
Till you found
The parts
That are alright

It Never Quite Fits

I am a seamstress
Constantly trying
To piece together this mess
Piecing my words and thoughts
Into something
Resembling art

I join ideas at the seams
Bust them
And re-stitch
Desperately trying
To make my dreams

I place and replace
Places I've been
People I've seen
Thoughts and memories
Trying to make
The version of me
I want to be

Someday They'll Know

Constantly
Thinking, thinking, thinking,
Trying to piece together
The fractured bits
Of your mind.
You know what they are
But you can't figure out how
To get them as far
As your mouth.
They always get stuck
Along the route
Never showing how grand
They truly are.
Like Wonderland,
Never quite able
To come with Alice
Out of the hole
To show the world

Making Sense of It

Art is
Us desperately

Trying to piece together
The life we see

Trying to say
What our mouths
Can't explain

Trying to show
How we feel
When we ourselves
Don't even know

Trying to capture
A moment in time
Before
It escapes from our minds

An I.V. of Ink

I write
As if
It will make, everything
Alright
Because maybe
It will help the voices
Not to fight

I write
In hopes the ink
Will somehow say
What I think
Even if I don't
Quite know what that is

I write
As I sometimes pray
Wishing that
It will make everything
Okay

I write
Because I need to
Get through
Another night

Own You

The tears keep coming
As you sit in the dark
Your thoughts keep humming
You don't know why
You tried to hide
But they are so sly
They find you first
And keep you away
Which makes you feel worse
And you lose reason to stay

Kill Us Softly
Alone at night
When nothings right
One thing with you
In your fight

A bottle
Full of fire

A needle
For a different feel

Another body
Their touch
Never enough

A knife
With steel
Cold as ice

Pick your poison
Numb the pain
Until
It is all that remains

Do Tears Fall?
If someone cries
Alone at night
And no one is there
To see the tears
Or how they breathe
If no one is awake
As they shake
If not,
Then
Does it even happen?

Just Like the Moon
You've taught me
To love the dark

Alone at night
I am free

All who know me
Are the stars

And because of you
Everyone else
Will stay afar

Forever Embrace
Hello loneliness
Wrap me up
In your arms
Keep me close
Away from people
That bring me harm
Alone at night
You embrace me tight
A constant companion
One to count on
Always near
You know my fears
And with them
You stay

What Are You?

Around and around
It's the same everyday
Oh why won't you go away?

A repeating refrain
In my brain
Always finding
A reason to stay

You've made yourself a home
And now I can't remember
Life with you gone

What Happened?
There is no peace
He is here

Always

Even when not

My friend fear
Sits with me

Like a rock

It's the only thing
That lives
In my heart

Now who is the Fool?
Real monsters don't hide
No
They are the ones
Who abide
In our beds.
Who take up space
In our heads.

They don't dwell
Outside the wall
For we invite them in
The moment
They flash a grin.
And we are so blinded
By their bright,
White, teeth
We refuse to believe
They could be a even thief,

Oh the shock
When we give them our hearts
And watch
As they pick them apart
Into more pieces
Than the stars

Invisible Scars
Everyone leaves a mark
On our hearts
I wonder if we knew
How the ones we leave looked
Would that change how we part?
Would we tread more gently?
If we saw how we could bruise?
Or would we cause
Even more abuse?

Unstably Stable
Oh the human heart
Is so incredibly strong
It can hold
So much
For so long
Or give
Even when
Its own self
Is struggling to live
It can break
Into a million pieces
And still wake
With a smile the next day
It can share
Countless bits
Of itself
And still care
About another soul.
Oh my dear,
What other creature
Is more capable
Than your seemingly unstable
Beautiful heart?

M

Oh how my heart misses you
You who came when I didn't want you to
I saw you and your brokenness
And it took my breathe away
At first, we were only surviving
But in the end I wished you could stay
I'm sorry I could not do more
And you had to go back to before
I wish that you were mine
Then I could at least
Make sure you're fine
But instead I sit here not knowing
Where next in life you'll be going
All I can do is hope and pray
That somehow, you are okay

My Reservoir of Ghosts
You see my heart
Wants to be whole
That is why
When it loses one part
I so easily cry
For all that is lost

With each new hurt
I also feel
All of the scars
That will never quite heal

The pain reminds me
Of all the things
I will never again find

Carry On

Why aren't you here?
Why am I, only left with tears?
You came and went so fast
What is the point if nothing lasts?
How did all I know is true
Disappear out of the blue?
Now all I can do is pretend
That I am okay, with this end

Alternate Realities
Dreams are where
All the lost go.
When this reality
Is too much to bear
I escape to sleep
And it is there
That I meet
All those
That I could not keep,
And for a bit we live
The life
That could've been
If only
Things were different

Faster
Always behind
Racing to keep up
But the words always slow to find
Moving on too soon
No one left to listen but the moon
So much to give
If only it weren't,
So hard to live

Falling
What am I doing
Sitting watching leaves blowing?
Like them. No place that I am going
I sit, feeling the cool breeze kiss
Wondering why, life feels amiss

Just Out of Reach
Sometimes you don't know
What you think
Your brain won't work
And when you are on the brink
Of something
You open your mouth
And choke
Laugh it off
For your life is a joke

But inside,
Your mind,

Screams

Because its' only
Dream

Is to know

Pet or Pest
Just remember
In a couple days
This won't matter
Don't let it get in your way
Take a minute
To sit with it
And feel
Know it's real

Then let go
No need for a show
Let it go
Like a stray cat
Don't feed it
And eventually
It won't come back

Here

Welcome my friend
I know it's been awhile
And you think any second I could end
But please don't let that fear
Stop you
From seeing what is here
Yes the good may go to fast
But you know
Nothing really lasts
So why are you sitting
Thinking of tears?
When that is not, what is right here?

There Will Be Some like This

Some days are full
Of kittens playing
And children singing
Coffee sipping
And rock climbing
Nothing exciting
But all worth living

And Some Like This
Somedays,
I am just afraid.
Of change
Of staying the same
Of loneliness
Of life always a mess
And somedays,
I am just tired.
With nothing
Left to say

And Still Others Like This

And some days are there
To remind you
Not to forget
This isn't it
Things will change
Your life
Will wax and wan
Nothing stays the same
And that's okay
It's what keeps us
Trying
It keeps us going
Knowing
That this isn't all we have
We can try again
When the alarm rings

Hello Friend
It's okay
To have nothing to say
I know you are worn
And your mind is all torn
So take your time
I've nowhere to go
I'll wait here with you
Till you find back your flow

Let the Sun Rise

I see you there, sitting alone
Thinking of how, the demon has grown
You wonder how, it got to this
And think back to, when ignorance was bliss
What if, you've gone too far?
Maybe this, is just who you are
What is the point, of giving a care?
Why not, just be friends with despair?
And now you welcome pain in
It's what you deserve, for your sin
But what if instead, of taking more pain
You used that energy, for your own gain?
I know it feels, like you'll never be free
This is just, who you will be
But why not, get up and try?
What if you're only, seeing a lie?
Maybe, what you think is right
And this is all, just an endless night
But the only way to know, if hope is gone
Is to get up, and try, to bring the dawn

Fleeting Like Fireflies
This low
Will pass
I know it seems
Like it may never
Really go
But nothing lasts
Forever

All we are
Is moments
And a better one
Is never far
If you just look
You will find one
In the smile
Of a child
Or of the moon

Yes they will fade
And you will search
For another
Cause all you can really do
Is build a reservoir
Of good moments

Slow Growing
Doing the same thing
Everyday
Thinking nothing of it
Then one day looking
Back, at what happened along the way
Just getting by
Doing what you must
Now look at what you made
And you didn't even try

Just Move

You don't have to
Decide now
There's a reason
They call it
A leap of faith
And it's not always
Necessary to leap
Sometimes just a hop
Or a step
Or even a stumble
Will get you
To where you need to go
Just try
And you might
End up surprised

Fresh Water
I only
Wanted to get my feet wet
But I enjoyed the cool rush
Of the water
And the surrounding beauty
Green and lush

I stayed
For longer than intended
And as the playful current tugged
I thought,
What's the harm
In riding it to the end?

Little Bit Pyro

Playing with fire
Is that what this is?
Watching flames crackle and hiss
More and more warmth on my skin

Feeling the heat kiss
Always yearning for more
Knowing the sparks
Can burn and scar
If this dance
Is taken too far

And asking myself
When the embers burnout
Will I be left
With warmth in my heart?
Or colder than the start
Inside and out?

I Guess Mama Warned Me

When I was a kid
I loved
To dip my fingers
In hot, melted, wax
And watch
As it hardened
Giving me shiny,
New fingertips.
Ignoring the burn
For that, captivating feel
New and almost
Beautiful

And now, I think
Loving you,
Was similar to,
Dipping my heart
In hot wax.
I was so taken
By the strange sensation
Of your loves embrace
A smooth, tough, shell
Almost comforting,
Once the wax cooled

And I willingly ignored
The bit of burn

xxxviii

That always came with you

But eventually
Like my fingertips,
My heart was dipped
One too many times.
And when the shell
Fell away
Something new stayed

The heat had formed
A new barrier,
Of rough and ugly callouses
That now fail to feel
Anything new

Careful What You Wish For
She fell in love
With the sun
And all the light and warmth
It showered on her
Everyday though
It went
In a dramatic flash
And she was left
With her cool, quiet, companion,
The moon
Always there to silently sit

But still
She craved the sun
Shiny and hot
She did not heed
All the warnings
And as she got closer
To the fire she so wanted
She eventually found herself
Blind and burned
No longer able
To even know
The soft, gentle, glow,
Of her moon

Creatures of the Dark
We are often
Like moths
Seeking light
We see
It is good and bright
But we make the mistake
Of giving our all to it
Even though
We truly
Belong to the night

Chipped Away

I watched as your words,
Like knives,
Carved beauty out of life.
So captured by your abilities
I didn't even care when,
Quite cool and sharp
They started cutting into me
For I trusted that as always
You were making, something more gorgeous
And it took me so long to notice
As you silenced my voice
And molded my body
That you were making a beauty
Solely for you
Because you did not have the capacity
To appreciate the fullness of me

Who are you?
She was like a cactus
A survivor
Full of a different beauty
Many who looked
Saw the prickly walls
And moved on
But
If you stayed awhile
And put in the work
You'd discover
The lovely interior
The harsh desert
Forced her to hide

Masterpiece

Who told you, to hide away?
Why don't you, let your spirit play?
I know it is buried, somewhere in there
What made you think, it was too much to share?
Why has the world, not learned its lesson?
Nothing good, comes from oppression
Don't we know, of the horrors brought
When we enslave, without a second thought?
We were all taught, of the giant mess
That comes, when people are suppressed
So why oh why, do we not see
The dangers, of suppressing inwardly?
Why don't we have the bravery,
To break from our own slavery?
The world may try, to put you in a mold
But you are the one, which lets it keep its hold
When will you see, you're not just a brain and
heart
You are in fact, a work of art
And art is not meant, to just please the eyes
It is worth so much more, than one may realize
Art demands, to be seen, felt, and heard
It can move people, without a single word
Not all, may understand its story
But that does not stop it
From showing its glory
So stop, repressing your soul, please

Keep growing, and soon, you'll be a masterpiece

Inner Beauty

If you cut a tree open
You will find its scars
More commonly known
As knots

Throughout its life
A tree loses branches
But this loss
Does not stop
Its growth

The tree simply
Continues its journey
Going over or around
The space the branch left
Letting nothing detract
From its magnificence

And eventually
You'd only know
Something was once there
If you cut it down
And found
The marks of loss inside

Looking at you now
So beautiful and whole

xlvi

It makes me wonder
If we cut you open
How many knots
Would we find inside?
What kinds of loss
Have you grown over?

Who is Worthy?

I have grown
To like being alone
In my space
No need for a face
Sometimes it's good
For me
To just be
I don't need to show
All my parts
For I am like
A collection of art
That not all would,
Appreciate to see
And it's okay
To make people pay
To see certain rooms
In my museum
For I have realized
The price
Of all of me,
Is infinity

Hand-Me-Downs of the Past
Sometimes when you go
To the places you've known
You'll realize
How much you've grown

You see
The people you knew
And who
You used to be
With them
And when you try
To slip that person back on
You realize
It fits just a little wrong
It's all
Just a smidge too small

So you'll hang it up
With the child hoodie memories
The dresses of regret
And the sweaters of days better

And maybe someday
You'll have the chance
To show it off, and say
Look here
It may not be
xlix

Quite your style
But I once too
Wore your size
And I understand
What you are growing through

The Right Reason

She's only five
But oh so alive
She dances around
In her dress and gloves
Picking weeds from the ground
And giving them
To everyone.
It's how she loves,
But her king and queen
Are too busy
To live in her dream
And they leave the flowers
To wilt.

The princess
Guesses
Not all
Can see her love
For it is so small,
So she stores it down
Saves it for a prince
To who it can be shown.

Time goes by
And she finds a guy
Who drinks up
All she has to give

But when he's taken
All her hoard
He finds himself
Bored.
And moves on

She ends up alone
All her magic
Gone
And she decides then
She will never again
Make her love,
Like pretty petals
To be dropped,
Or stored in a massive trunk
To be chopped,
No she would grow like ivy
Fast and strong
And when trimmed
Grow back, twice as long

Too Much of a Good Thing
We are taught
When we are young
All about
How to love.
We see it everywhere
In stories
In songs
And we learn
Of how
It is every souls yearn,
But what no one
Ever tells
Is how we can love so much,
That we lose ourselves
How too much of anything
Eventually kills
Even something so beautiful
And wonderful
As the people we love

Too Decadent, Too Deep

I was so starving
When I found you
So hungry
For a connection like ours
I didn't know
How to handle it
So I fell far
Into whatever we are
And got
So very
L
  O
    S
      T

Careful of the Sweet Tooth
Out of nowhere
There he stood
And for once
You had something
So very good
But it didn't last
As quick as sweet came
So did the rot
And you soon discovered
The man he was not

Nobody Deserves That
She watches
As he moves
And tries not to feel
His fingers
Like matches

Wondering how
This is happening now
Just an innocent kiss
How does that,
Lead to this?

Or This
Lovers
Cherish the night
But not I
For darkness covers
All of his sins
And the terrors
They always bring

Don't You Deserve More?
Why girl
Do you keep this up?
You once were full
But it was a trap
You want it back
To how it was
But the fact
Is, it wasn't love

She Made it

He was like a summer drought,
Suffocating and seemingly endless
So she found solace in another.

He was like refreshing autumn,
But autumn turns to winter
And winter is icy and deadly.

Winter also, tells you to fly or die
So with the promise of new growth
She set off, in search of warmth.

Fly Away

She takes it in stride
All the yelling and lies
It's the same every time
And she hides her head and cries
Why, oh why, is this my life?
What did I do to deserve this strife?
She gives herself five
Then she dries her eyes
Cause she knows, she's gotta continue the fight
And she does all she can
And hopes its right
As she makes it through another night

He pulls down his sleeves
There's no blood at least
He wonders when next
He'll see the beast
He asks himself if he's better off dead
Than living this life filled with dread
But he knows
That if he goes
There'll be no one left to soften the blows
His sister can't handle it all alone
So he picks himself up
And puts on a grin
Cause he knows he can't
Let the devil win

She tries not to cringe
As he touches her skin
She feels so dirty
Oh why can't he hurry?
How did this become her life?
All she wanted was to be a wife
And now she hides
Alone and cold
No one would believe her
Even if she told

I know their stories
And so I pray
Give them wings to fly away
Don't make them live this another day
Grant them the strength to break away

It doesn't work
They all still stay
Why doesn't God lift them from this fray?
Don't they deserve to be okay?

But then I watch
And I see
They are so much stronger than me
They can break away
From this pain
And see

lxi

What else they have to gain
They have the strength
To be free
As long as
It is what they want to be

Help Themselves
I sit
And watch
Them go through shit.
I see
Her in the pit
With the company
Of a bottle
Taking her
Full throttle
And yet I sit

I watch
Her on the ladder
With her friend
The dagger
Guessing how
It will end
And still I sit now

I behold
The hole
He left
And the tears
Of her darkened soul
And still I sit
Like a lump of coal

I've known
Their lives
And what's shown
In their eyes
So why
Must I sit?

For You
I watch you
As you breathe
So silent
You barely move
This state
Brings me ease
There is almost peace
No weight,
Of the world
On your face
For a few hours
You stay.
And everything, is okay

For Me
Sweet sleep come to me
In this life you set me free
I have you when it's too much to carry
Why must you be so temporary?

How to Be Free
It was not right
This "it" I couldn't see
Everything
Was what it seemed to me
So I went
To the endless sea
Trying so hard
To be free

But the "it"
Followed
Me to the beach
And this lesson
"It" did teach

"It"
Was something
I could not flee
Twas not a face
Or a place
No "it"
Was a part of me

Never Knew
There she was
Late nights
Dreaming with the stars
Not quite right
But not even she
Knows it

Then
Life moves
In a direction
She never
Thought to choose

She races
To keep up
With whatever
This is
And through it
She finds
What was amiss

Just Wait, It'll Rise

It was the right color
But the wrong shade
Which no one knew
Until it started to fade

And in its place
Came more hues
Beautiful and bright,
But still not right

But these too
Went away
And left
The most beautiful blue
And right away they saw
That this one was true

Last Few Moments
I have a theory
That the end of our lives
Is like a sunset
All fiery and red
Here one moment
And the next, dead.

It's something incredible
To be remembered
And even if
No one is there
To see it
Like the sunsets
It still happened
One of a million
But still beautiful and grand

Lessons from Above

Why can't we
Be more like the sky
When things are heavy
Cry
But also don't be
Afraid to shine
For life may try
But it cannot hide
Your light for long
As long, as you keep
It going strong

Revitalization

Sometimes
A storm must rage
Tears must fall
Like rain

And you must scream and yell
Speak your soul's pain
Roar
Like the thunder

Let the hurt
Tear you down
Like a hurricane

Let yourself drown
Just a little though
For once the storm recedes
You will be given
The chance you need
To grow

Stronger and better
Than you were before
Because the storm
Shook you to your core

Black Holes of Beauty
Eyes
Oh the beauty they hold
The sorrow
The joy
The stories untold
And when emotion
Is too much to carry
They release it for you
In trails of tears
And then just as quickly go back
To hiding your fears
Your gorgeous eyes
Truly do
Show a glimpse
Of that endless soul

Glimpses Inside
Your eyes
Are like stained glass windows
Sometimes appearing
Fractured and dark
But when light
Shines through
They are so vibrantly blue
So beautiful to behold
Full of stories untold
Leaving me wishing I could make
The sun shine on you
All the days

Missing the Stars in Our Eyes
How to be
Alive again
Like we were
When we were kids?
What are we missing
That we had then?
What thing of life
Did we forget?
What did we gain
For this price,
Of getting by
And trying to survive?

Remember?
You
Are alive
Something so easy
To forget
When you survive.
Forget the sun and moon
Forget summer breezes
Forget the roars and whispers
Of water
Forget the uncontrollable laughter
Of a child
Forget all the things
That help you thrive

Snippets about You

You will never feel at home
If you can't first
Be comfortable
In your own skin

A glimpse in the mirror
And I see
A stranger
But only to me

Do We Ever Truly Find It?
Home
A place that some
Have never known

Made for weary
Hearts to come

A place
Not always

Sometimes home
Is a name or face

But always
Something

Whether had or not
That we will yearn for

To fill
An ever hungry spot

What Once Was
This house is full
Of ghosts

Ghosts of people
And the memories
They have

Ghosts of tears
Cried in the night

Ghosts of words
Yelled in a fight

But also
Ghosts of laughter
Lingering in the air

In the holes in the wall
You can see ghosts,
Of people who cared

So let us toast
This house
And all the ghosts
Of the people just trying
To live

lxxix

M II

Please stay with me
And happy we will be
Not perfect
But I'll make it worth it

Take my love
It's what I can give
And even if
We go our ways
I'll remember this
All the days

I give you a piece
Of my heart
To stay with you
When it is dark
If I am not there
Please remember
I'll always care

M III

There you've done it
Given away
A piece of your heart
Knowing someday
It won't stay
All too soon
It'll be taken away
You'll be left with an ache
Not quite the same
As heartbreak
And you'll hope
That piece
Is enough
To get them through
A life so rough

Just Wait for Summer
And just like that
It's over
Like a warm day
In the middle of winter

It was a change
That I always new
Wouldn't last

All too soon
It would be in the past

Sweet and short
It left you
Wishing for more

But knowing
It was gone
And all you could do
Was move on

Even More Things We Say
It happens so fast
I go and get attached
Even as I'm doubting
It will last

And then the parting
Comes about
And I tell myself
It's all good
Just memories
To be put on a shelf
But as much
As I say I can
The past moments
Don't make it out of my hand
I know those times
Are long gone
But a part of me
Just won't move on
Even as I say
I've been good all along
And you never did belong
I still hold on

The Things We Tell Ourselves
I told myself
I would not write
About you
For then it would be real

I told myself
Not to feel
Too much toward you
As if
Somehow saying it
Would make it true

I wonder if
If I hadn't tried to fool
My heart with rules
Would I have known
How much I would miss you?

Almost Immortal

I wonder what you would think
If you knew
How I write about you

Would you understand
That I write
To process
And make things alright?
That I write my life,
The wins and losses

Would you be flattered?
Because when I write
It becomes real
And I have finally
Let myself feel

See if I put you in ink
It means
You made an impact
On my existence
You made your way
Into my brain
To stay
Even after you're gone

Musings
A moment
That is all this is
We make more of it
But when you stop
And think
You realize
How
We are now
And in the blink of an eye
It can all subside
And you may choose
To watch it slip away
Or you may seize
The fading day

Or maybe
I am wrong
And we are more
Than a moment.
All I know
Is here I sit
Writing away
A little life
On this page

Memories
Don't make a sound
It drips to the ground
Most stories are made
By ink sinking
Into the page
But this pours down
As the story's scratched out
Now all can see
What life can be

More Memories
For every scar
That you see
On my heart
There are three

What a Klutz
She was a clumsy being
And if you looked you could see
The nicks and bruises
On her body
From the tripping and falling

What you don't know
Is, that body,
Just mirrors her heart.
For she too often falls
In the wrong place
Or time

And the bruises and scars
On her heart
Are there to remind her
That love hurts
Love is hard
But still she doesn't learn
She just keeps falling
Oh that foolish, clumsy, heart

Made for Waves
I fell for
Your beautiful mind
With trying to find
The bottom of it

And I was so busy
Trying to dive deep
That I didn't see
'Twas not the water for me

I was so intrigued
With your deep blue pools
That I tried to forget
I'm a saltwater girl

For it was just so refreshing
To feel the crystal-clear blue swirl
But once I stepped back,
For the water, was just, too cool
I remembered

All the rivers and lakes
As lovely as they are
Could never satisfy me
Like the deep green sea

For Poetry
Why am I so drawn to you?
Perhaps
It is because like me
You do not
Always make sense
To everyone
You might not quite
Seem complete
So not all
Can appreciate
The beauty
Of your jagged edges
And fragmented ideas

Bibliophile
Stories
Her forever companion
First
She found them
As a paper friend
Escaping
To worlds of pretend
Hungry for more
Than their spines
Could provide

Then
She discovered
The best stories
Are alive
And those individuals
Are what makes her
Every morning
Want to rise

My Letter

Oh beautiful being
So alone and dealing
With all the demons
I want you to know
That I see what you're feeling
I see the hurt and the pain
You wonder if life is in vain
I have been where you are
I know the story of that scar
I've used that mask
And I know, you would remove it
If someone would just ask
That song that you sing
I know the feelings it brings
I know who you are
And I wanted to say
Thank you, for living this life today
I know it is hard, and you are afraid
But you do not realize, you are so brave
I want you to know, you will make it through
And thank you, for doing what you had to
And handling what life threw at you
Thank you, for all the mistakes
And going on, when you wanted to break
Most of all, please keep living
For you do not realize the gift you are giving
And I'm not talking about to the people you see

I'm referring, to the person you'll be
Keep breathing, keep going, it'll get better
I know, cause I'm here to write you this letter

Human Experiences
You don't know me
But I wanted to say
That I saw you today
Hurrying along
Like you woke up wrong
Again

I saw the look of pain
When you tripped on the crack
And the embarrassment
Covered with a laugh

And in that moment
I could truly see
How you
Were no different from me

Blindly Forward
Just trying
To figure out
Figure out
Figure out
What exactly
This is all about
Feeling lost
And wishing that
You knew the cost
Of choices you make
But there is no award
For when you manage
To take a step forward
You just keep stumbling
Wondering
Hoping
That you are going
The right way

Just Blowing Air
I'm so tired
Of not knowing
Of losing my fire
Tired of trying
For something
To keep it growing
Wondering if
I'm just chasing smoke
And sooner or later
It will just make me choke

Sail Away

The waves keep crashing into me
The water's been making it harder to breathe
I could pull up my anchor and be lost at sea
What would it feel to finally be free?

But then I remember
That lost is not free
It might feel it at first
You can drift as you please
And feel nothing
But the sun and the breeze

But the storms will return
And you will learn
You do not want
To weather them alone

And you wonder why
You pulled the line
And left your home

Now you're too far away
And all those left in the bay
Feel the waves harder
Because you did not stay

If only you'd realized

xcviii

That you were a buffer
You decided to leave
And now they all suffer
But still none more than you

If only you knew
That you had something to lose
That you would not end up free
But instead
Taken by the sea

What's Your Secret?
Remember when
You would lay at night
And say you couldn't do it again?
When you would scream and cry
And wonder why
You couldn't die?
When the stars in the sky
Were the only ones
Who truly saw
Behind your eyes?
And all I knew
Was you weren't quite right
But I wanted so badly
To believe the lies
That you were fine

I'm sorry for then
I didn't understand
But I do now

And I'm asking you how
Did you get as far
As where you are?
Because I too
Am now familiar
With all the stars
And I need to know

c

How to be okay
How to live these days

Because if you
No longer wish to go
I know that I too
Can find a way
To stay

Only You
Solitude
A word which for each
Brings a different mood

For some the idea
Brings much fear
Not knowing how to deal
When only they are near
Always finding something
To drown the noises
Only they can hear

Yet for others
It is solace.
Safety and comfort,
Can only be found in this place
The only time to just be
And not have to wear anther face

Bunker Down
Maybe it's better
To live in my head
A place
Where no one is dead
Where all will be
In harmony
Somewhere I can predict
And my whole being
Can exist
Safe from everything
But me
My
Own
Worst
Enemy

Not Real?
Mind racing
Heart pounding
Can't keep up
Thoughts chasing
Make it stop
No avail
Pull yourself
From this hell

Build a Back Way Out
You've hit it
A rock bottom
For now

You've fallen apart
And don't know how
To put it right

So sit
For a minute
In this low
And figure out
One thing

Just one
To build and grow

Right now you know
This is a place
You don't want
To come back to

So find something
For you
A way
To make sure
Even if
cv

You come back here
You won't stay

Making it into Some Thing
You don't know
What you think
Or how you feel
So you put it down
In paint or ink
And hope that somehow
It'll say what you can't
And help you heal

Rewinding Minds

Do you ever feel
Like your mind
Continuously rewinds
The same tracks?
When you think you're done
You find yourself back
To number one

Do you feel like
A skipping record?
And you can't figure out
How to make it play
So it goes around
All the way
Trying to stop singing
The same old tunes
And just when you do
They start ringing
Again through you

Don't Loiter

I wish you would pay
For the space
You take up in my head
It's not the place
I want you to be

Honestly
I'd do better
If you weren't anywhere
Especially
Right below my hair

Just think
Of the money I'd make
From all the space you take

Or what if instead
You left
And someone or something else
Filled my head

Someone who cared
Who knew and wanted
To be there

Pruning of You
What if all the pieces
Of your heart that you lose
Are just making room
For someone
To give you for once
More than
Just a fragment
Of theirs

Always Stitching
I am constantly
Trying to reconcile
All the parts of me
To accept and know
All the people I've been
So I can learn to grow
Into someone I want to be

Grafting
I guess if you found
Someone who really
Gave you their heart
It would be more than enough
To patch up
All the holes
From the pieces
You gave away
To only get trampled on the ground
All of those missing fragments
Would make room
For your heart to be
Even more whole

Thinning the Forest
And you will learn
That some are meant to leave
At first
Your heart will grieve
And yearn
To fill the empty space
That they left
In their place
But you will eventually find
That all along you were meant
To fill the room left behind
With you

Cryovolcanos
You can't
Keep it frozen forever
You were made to thaw
If you weren't
Heat wouldn't be
Where you're drawn
The ice
Serves a purpose
To show off
Your beauty and worth
And the heat
Wishes to make you melt
So in you, it can drown

Sometimes though
The fire is too strong
And we evaporate
And are gone

But we always
Reform
Into something
The old flame
Would not dare touch
For it could not withstand
The new flood

Thank You

Thank you, for not giving a damn
Because of it, I am who I am
Thank you, for always choosing you
Now I know, what not to do
Thank you, for always running away
It made me learn, when to stay
I want you to know
You helped me grow
And even with, all the pain you did bring
I wouldn't go back, and change a thing
You might have thought, you were breaking me
But instead, you were merely, setting me free

Who Lost Who?
How I believed
All of your lies
And how I grieved them
Every time
But I eventually saw
What was wrong.
It was a long road
Letting you go
So forgive me
When I am not keen
To accept your tries

You say I've grown
And flown
So much further
Than you'd like
If you didn't want me
To fly this free
Then you shouldn't have pushed me
From your twisted tree

Who Has the Power?
Please
Stop
All the lies
Can't take it
Almost better to die

But no
That is not your end
You take it
And then my friend
You rise
From their fire

That look
In their eyes
When they see you fly
And you
Will no longer cry

What's the Worth?

She watched them
As the belt fell

And once again
With that yell

She silently learned
To be good as gold

And do whatever
She was told

Until
She decided pain

Was nothing
Compared to the gain

Building Strength

I see you there
Little one
Who shouldn't have a care
What did they do
To make you so scared?
That haunted look,
Do you realize what they took?
They gave you a weight
To carry along
And you welcomed it
For you did not know
It didn't belong
But little one
Let me tell you
As they gave
What was not true
They forgot
How you are brave
How all of this
Would make you strong
And one day
You'll prove them wrong

The Gift of You

Will you come
And lay with me?
We don't have to speak
Just be
Or if you'd like
You can tell me about
Your day, your week,
Your month, your year
Tell me about
All you care for
And all you fear
Tell me about
The last time
You were truly
Happy
Or you could, just
Not say a word
Some moments are best
Undisturbed
Either way
If you choose to say
Everything
Or nothing at all
You will have shown me
A part of you
And that
Will have made my day

cxx

ACKNOWLEDGMENTS

Firstly, I want to thank my mom. I know you had no idea I was making a book and so technically you couldn't help me with it, but I doubt I would be here today if it hadn't been for you. You always encouraged in me, a love for reading, and always lent an ear, to listen to, whatever crazy dreams or ideas, I had.

I also need to thank Bridget, my Illustrator, best friend, and "wife", for always listening to and encouraging the crazy dreams and ideas I have now. You have always been there for me and I can't imagine my life without you.

Thanks to Luke, Patrick, and Timm, for actually reading my work when I asked you too and providing feedback, whatever amount you gave me was greatly appreciated.

Thanks to Margaret, for thinking my poetry was good and telling me I needed to publish my work from the very beginning.

And thanks to anyone who gave encouragement along the way, I don't know if you believed I would actually write the book, but if you didn't, it didn't really show, and now here we are. So thank you.

ABOUT THE AUTHOR

Read the poems. They'll tell you more about me
than this page ever could.